WHITE CITIES

For Elizabeth

with many good wishes

Ben

April 03

WHITE CITIES

BEN MAZER

BARBARA MATTEAU EDITIONS

Cambridge, Massachusetts

1995

Some of the poems in this book have appeared
in LIFT, ATELIER, and ENGLYNION.

Cover and title-page illustration by Frank Parker

PRINTED IN THE UNITED STATES OF AMERICA

To
ERIC DAVIS

Contents

Fountain

Think of nothing, do not betray the spell,
a coin is tossed under your rug, don't look,
in the dark, mysteries contained in orbit,
jangling odors, voices in embryo,
a love inevitable, clothed in human sweetness,
clouds mired in gilded groans suspended,
a stench as of the birth of cities,
of the ruptured paths of angels' feet,
black, cloaked, a jet of seasprayed coins.

Hospital Song

Back from the wars,
Without my wares,
But lying here,
Not quite sure where,
Permitted this,
Calm to the eyes,
A world of shadow,
Suited for widow.

Burnt smells no longer
In nostrils linger,
Yet others attack,
Slightly septic;
Difference is
Most wise of laws
And here no hurry,
But sanctuary.

Preludes

I

Morning wakes— in shattered alleys
light blames beyond breadth of memories,
retaliating origin in the mind...
to broken steps of stone that sing
and wink beneath the latticed height
of closure that remarks a golden coin...
to lift a voice bent in the void
where laundry and laundry meet
on lines
between the window holes of street and street...

II

At the end of a dead street
In noon's obscurity
Purple portal of stone
Is tided of the world
That you are instant in.

A Visitor

The flier, at the Wicklow manor,
Stayed throughout the spring and summer,
Mending autos in the drive,
Reprising time-old moods of love
In the limbs of country lasses
Who wondered where he gave his kisses.

Expert at geography
And mathematic, for no fee
He made the summer days pass faster
And taught them how to see the pasture
With their own eyes. The books he read,
Handled till their cloth was frayed,
Years afterwards upon their shelves
Lay early, central to their lives.

Paristu

Up in his room, who would have thought to see
The trappings of a budding architect
All laid out neatly; ready to begin
Some enterprising project, let us in
To see his Frank Lloyd Wright stones on the floor
—The chiefest prize of summer work he'd done
Restoring, down south; imitating palms
Indigenous to that environment,
They focused sunlight, mythic in their gaze
Amidst piles of his dirty underwear.
I wondered to what fortune he was heir,
Who need withstand our presence in the noon
With all his projects ready to begin,
And suddenly the sunlight out of tune.
The splayed buds of his Humboldt mary jane
Distorted seconds in a plastic bag
From which their sweet aroma filled the air
As nymphs may be seen dancing through a fence.
He acted like he didn't have a care
As Paristu, indifferent and aloof,
Told him that we could go, or we could stay.
He invited us to climb onto the roof
And anteceded us with water pipe.
The emblem of his room, deep in our day
Was fountain of our consciousness and slow
That sought through idle impulse to be free.
Over the bay, ungrateful as a crab,
—Whose voyages are planned beyond the will—
Fluttering as a mountain or a flag
High in the sun's attentions, sky's parade,
Impelled to adoration of the sea,
Leaped the motif of our obscurity.
Leaves blow, and we cannot be sure where.

Biography

Your Japanese, your Oriental silks;
Your eyes tattooed with sun, and beer, and sea;
We anchored lazy in the afternoon
Wavering our memory in sun screens.
Not far, crowds climbed the golden boulevards;—
A sail is slip of love our noon ravines.

A Traveller

In a strange country, there is only one
Who knows his true name and could turn him in.
But she, whose father too was charged with murder
And, innocent, went to the electric chair,
Believes in him, convinces him to trust.
It is the tropics where they make their tryst.
They sip refreshing drinks beside a terraced
Pool where he is thought to be a tourist.
To clear his name, and find who killed his pal,
In a dark passage he finds hope and will.
What once had seemed exotic now seems near
Because he wished to be her prisoner.

Madrid

On the boulevards of Madrid
A single fountain dreaming
Is wakened in your sleep.

First, the shirts in the windows,
And then the coin in the mirror.
A single fountain dreaming.

I'll show you all my changes,
Youth of dust and ravines.
Day without witness or end—

Ice cream, coins, a fountain.
Your lapel shining at noon
With noone near you.

April

Imagine the gatekeeper of a hole the size of a small fist in a pointed slat fence along a side street, a back road not far from and parallel to the main street in a Town, the kind of neighborhood that inspires confidences. Crabgrass et les cloches des fleurs overgrow from beneath the slats so that on another day, alone, one might have guessed. Part magician, part master of ceremonies, (the gatekeeper) slyly solicits interest in a side show comparable in inspiration to the lemonade stands of little children. Fake diamonds, bedsheet turbans, mixtures of mud and pigment, gigantic cardboard tickets, an old card table for the magic cups. An open chest of costumes that only children could wear with such seriousness, alabaster pearls, the laughing voices of the dancers, those beauties, his little helpers, create the illusion of new acquaintances, not without being in a foreign possession. Good business, they fetch for him his garlands, which giggling or striking murderous poses they obediently tie to the thighs of his "over-alls." Really, this is no way to pass a spring afternoon, without having eaten and in the company of strangers!

Lines Written in the Adams House Library

Time is passing, we are aging.
Nights we rest, in sudden flight
the increments of our time off
from strained and steering afternoons
purloining peer-loined walls
resounds and lifts; we're reached.
If we are god—
this couch is all my love for thee,
and banks the halls of my ideals,
the emblem of the bonds we've shared,
no matter turned side to the light.
Aye, lift a leg of lamb for me
and saints you know it turns out right,
black stockings puddled to the floor,
the guard has got to watch the door.
(I say, we've tried that one before!)

The dames at Harvard all dress well,
boyfriends good at show and tell,
best on sofas do they shine,
doors shut best for passing time.

To suck a finger is no good
if it's not sucked blatantly rude.
At least, white stockings only contrive a whim
to see, and feel, and taste her quim.
Just an inch, rosy at the knee,
but her face looks like hamburger, and stray!
What's said beneath the clock as it chimes:
Her tale is in an envelope.

*

Their Shelley and their Keats they bare,
but their Byron is most fair!

*

I have got new shoes of foal,
dressed up just like Rbt. Lowell!

*

Seeing faces familiar,
Walking home I blindly stare.
What spires go turning in flight there?

L.F.D.

How perfectly I felt your heart in mine,
Familiar the station I had never seen,
Falling the shadows through which you approached,
Distance and the approaching now all one.

Brief as Radio Signal

Brief as radio signal, lover's kiss,
Dissolving distance, sanctifies the face:
Beneath the talkless mingling of the lips
Is conversation of two shadow laps.
The hand is paper, authorizing release
Of the would-be traveller behind the eyes,
Which had been gesture hiding the desire
So long withheld that it had turned to fear.
In a strange country, white beneath the sun,
Ghost in the form of its entrusted mission,
The heart finds meaning in the foreign tongue,
Who for the first time sees another one,
Immediate now, no longer through the window
That had contained, yet first invited view.

Rendezvous

The smell of irony... bitter with delight,
Is love which turns its colors in the breeze
Of summer nights, freshly arrived at tables
Outdoors, still tinged with glances from the mirror.
This rendezvous no others can recount,
Passers-by, is portable of pulses
Which beat thick with the instigation of trees
And fragrances, theatrical, of floodlights.
Separate voice and mask, no other speaks
But that which bargains for a dim content,
The drowning failure for the revolving doorway,
Beyond the temporary still piety of leaves.

J.O.Y.

Just as you said, we'd be apart
for a long time, and yet I feel
you're here. In fact, I often dream
how simply after all this time
then like a dream, remeeting you
would know our secret without words.
Astonish me, remembering coins or pearls
time buried in furthest latitudes,
effaced and unmappable souths, your pledge
which I can never leave nor translations extinguish,
familiar, beyond motion or even stillness.

Legend

The shadows of the flowers are nothing.
No mind can enter their silhouettes on the wall
But asks itself if it is borderless.
Dropping, without name, into its substance
It is the blossom of the heart's condition;
A stillness projected into emotion
Nursed far beyond the prospect of repair.

Matins

I am a jew, a chamber,
where light flows in,
whose tower beats with birds,
turned on the world
through light and time.
If Schubert is an opalescent jewel
whose iridescent purples bleed and writhe,
evaporate, transform within
the chamber of our time,
then what remains
at my heart's core
is white, constant, and hard.

The streets remain photogravures
of Paris in de Musset's time
and hopes are harboured in the light,
the same, that dances in the air.

Though gulls may spread their wings
within the light of my heart's tower,
the substance which they fly in,
through which streams the coming of our time,
the presence of all that's made from what
once was, has still its hard white core
part in another time.

Evening

The horn of the hunt
has discovered you,
In the bathtub—
Infant century!

*

This old house,
leaves that fall,
all are gone
over the sea.

*

That game behind glass
which features yourself,
is all that we have
of the old love.

Novel

In the grey factory streets of London, Italy, Spain,
We met in the morning of our lives
In the hours that we stole from poverty itself
Amidst the debris of Desolation
In the hours that life stole from us.
In California or Florida or Hawaii
I knew her as child,
when we played under the palms and beneath ranch fencing
on the sidewalk pavement or the tar of the street
looking at pebbles and ants in the fresh sunlight
not far from the sea;
        her pink or aqua or lavendar shirt
            smelled clean of her soft tawny skin
                when she was young.
I loved her then for the dignity she showed
            in our small world.
She grew up in a town unlike mine,
where her innocent pious eyes
were bathed in the soft and warm breezes and scents
        of coconuts, papaya, macadamia, jasmine,
            orange blossoms, lavendar.
She walked softly, with balled feet.
I followed her down the street in my childish dreams,
        watched her board the yellow schoolbus
            and there caught a glimpse of her noble suffering.
        I walked in the emptied boulevards
            in the ocean's breeze,
        and up to the old lady's,
            where I was given crackers.
            . In the plaza
She giggled in conference with her friend,
        the one without her magical beauty,
            around whom she was the queen.
I sensed them looking at me,
the friend smiling and loving me generously,

wanting me for her friend.
They snickered together at the transparent poser,
        until he left,
making it clear to me in subtle ways
          with blank eyes, staring and bored,
          sighs, a tilt of the chair,
          quick confiding smiles, between themselves,
          quicker than the unseeing ignored one,
          his face falling in intuited rejection,
          which he played off condemnably as jaded
            and arrogant boredom;
I waited and smiled faintly
        with mounting delight,
          shyness, hope,
            delirious elation,
      My nostrils full of all the reckless
          and gentle sensations of
almond, palm, dates, lavender, figs, hibiscus,
dolphin, lemons...
      She looked away from their table...
         towards me...
       not once *at* me...
      My head swam from her dignity...
At last he got up to leave.
They smiled, as though taking each other's hands.
      She looked ill, for a moment truly alone.
      I wanted to save her.
Her friend would have done anything, as my accomplice.
Her friend, the homely and fat one,
chosen to help me mend her broken heart.
In my dreams
     the three of us danced amidst pools of
          fountaining water.
     Jessica danced the highest.
     I next.
     and Carolyn below us.

The three of us had love to save the world.
Why did she grow up in a town where
her voice could never be heard.

Boardwalk

Eternal elements incarnated in brass
this epoch take the singular trumpet's shape
that styles our thoughts and hurries us along
before ballooning into popcorn in the air.

The edges of the mustaches we pass forth
into the streamlined resonance of our day
have drunk the phonograph's recorded lemonade
and piled pebbles on concrete in the shade.

The lion in the sun whose burning tongue
licks at the muscled banners of our joy
insidiously draws out the jealous glimpse
of progress as its residue is drained.

Avalon

Stone— as of leaf— the angle satisfies,
Ascent— whose oriental tapestries
Adorn, conclamant, your weaved shadowed light—
Blossomed, retribution falters bright.
Altars— what pathways these conceal
Within the pearly harvest that you file—
Imitation buries to unspoil
That wound which I wound seaward to be near,
Unparted shadow you may ever hear.

Departure

I'm ready for that great life of adventure that has always been the ultimate goal of all this. You understand— mystical mornings, divine coincidences— a frailty of circumstances. O mecca! Each morning I shall rise on the tail of rare perfumes, bedraggled and bewildered,— a carousel of innocent windows, slave-driven by eternity! And this shall be nothing new— every ancient and eternal mystery shall be uncovered... Let this serve as a herald for that which in the main now follows like a herd of camels appearing on the horizon thundering towards me.

The Garden

One day I went to see my love,
For I knew that she would be
Seated in a garden green,
Her earthly form to speak to me.

I prepared to speak to her.
Gently did I walk to her,
Underneath the large oak tree
Where she sat afraid of me.

What do you want? she asked of me.
Nothing that you'd keep from me.
Then she said to go away.
Then her spirit fled the day.

Then weeping I did sit beside
An infant under the blue sky.
Then I hung my head with shame,
For my memory knew her name.

Spring

In the spring of a new year, burdened by wearisome chores,
Emptying dead history professors' apartments of wares,
I look out through the window at the still world out of doors.

The clear blue sky, the clouds, the cool and floating air,
The dogwood, white and blooming, the children on the grass,
The three empty garden chairs, all fill the loved heart with fear.

The time when we loved, my darling, seems worlds and worlds away,
And the memory of that power we held in each other's arms
Will not be returned to us tomorrow or today.

For now is time of work, the dulling, numbing pain
Of growing old beneath the weight of sensible plans;
There is no time for seeing what in innocence we have seen.

The square, brick walls of the entrance of the path to the hall
                     from the street
Guard part of their existence from motion and from sight,
Continual like love's wisdom, intuited by the heart.

The empty path round the garden, which in another time
We might have felt free to walk on in mutual, expanding joy,
Is signal of what is promise, of what is yet ours to claim.

Dialogue from "A Wedding in the House of..."

Jimmi the butler: I serve you this mine glory
                My velvety plume drapes
                Keep me "warm by you".
        Phil: Aw shit, Jimi, you drink the bloody "Moloko plus".
                hah... I'm goin' ta need ya later.
        Jimi: Right boss. (gulps drink)
    Blondie: Hi, Jimi.
        Jimi: Man, you gonna freeze in them "Hefties". Dig
                these clouds.
    Blondie: mmmmmm
        Jimi: An' we blend in with the curtain too...

                * MEANWHILE *

            Phil is drunk.

        Phil: Hah hah haw!..
        Bill: onna monna peia i yi yi yi yi yi yiiiiii
        Phil: FUCK YOU ASSHOLE
        Bill: C R A S H !
        Phil: AAAAAAAAARGH!

                * * *

Pena Doola: I'm so sorry honey
                no... I'm so sorry big boy
                no... I'm really sorry kid
                        C'est la vie
                    no no I...
                    I... Oh God!
                I'm so sorry! Oh God,
                        will you ever forgive me?
    Brand X: I loved you.
    Chorus: I'm singing in the rain...

* Meanwhile in the backyard...

Red and Blue boy: I love to watch the seagulls flying through the mist.
My, it's chilly out here. I can't see yellow. That's
why I'm called Red and Blue boy. I wish I could remember
what my old house looked like.
Fish: Yeah. I love cold clammy Gloucester beach days.
Miss Boob: Come on kids. Back on the bus.
Red and Blue boy: Hey, the bus is yellow!
Fish: Yeah, but it's too misty to really see it. Everything's
grey. etc.
Boy: It's blue.

*The Bus leaves them off in the familiar town of Rockport,
where everyone is at least a little drunk. The candystore girl offers
directions to the nearest bar for all newcombers.

People from Texas roads and Virginia keg parties are cool
and in my mind and people gotta go and piss or look at pretty basic
"island art".

This one stupid old bald guy sits down on a rock, sees
the only local cop, dumbo, and starts writing a letter with melted
butter on. He addresses it thus:

Dear Marie,
Scream into pillows when you think of it all.
I loved you as all do each and I will soon soon you know. GLUMPH
CHROMP DRINKYUK.
Remembers drinks by the cafe at the hotel exete r
(actually it was only one drink)
Well, bye bye. See you in London maybe.
Yours truly,
Dream Grumph

Somewhere in France, residents got letters on Monday
morning describing their quaint cottages. How odd.
The mustachioed old shoemaker got a telegram:

"Make me a shoe of gold's leather and I may travel the world."

Shoemaker left candles on the sill and when Red and Blue boy looked through the window it was colored in blue or dark.

*Lou stood in the kitchen. Sunlight shone through the red and orange and yellow sun curtains. To Lou it must have been about 1946. What a shame to be ugly as Peter Parker and have raisins on one's belly. He was teaching someone how to buy atomic stocks and bonds. Buildings rotated in his head.

Wendell Street in Winter

A whole, huge, complicated world
Of New England rooftops, snow-covered,
Trees, and houses
Fills my window where I stare
Out of the blue-curtained darkness
Like a photographer photographing
The white separate world of wonder
Outside the images of sleeping
Which wander through the dark
Like sleepwalkers over cinema cradles,
Keepers of love letters,
And histories of failures.
The sheer unwitnessed vista of this perception,
Untainted surface of unfigured deeds,
Of patterns of possibility and recurrence
Which are ever dark in their unknowing, and in
The possibility of some new and darker creation,
Relieves the letter-writer of his burden,—
His special need to qualify the relationships
Of silence, centuries his fathers crawled across.
Who could make use of the full extent of these roofs?
Running, and jumping, and sitting,
A platform for dialogues,
This is their legacy!
Constructions taken apart, commemorating refreshment!
Scaling their angles
At bird-sport height mirroring the trees'
Black negation of time
Which can never be duplicated,
They jump to conclusions!
The names of their families unravel
In the unkempt yards.
Chimneys smoke white dust of snow,
Blown across the fidelity of broken charm.

Passage

The brilliant points of lives upon the shore
Sidereally reveal the plummet depth,
The traveller's calendar. Surface to the eye
And mute to the heart, they scurry in yards and basements,
Readying dawn for a prisoner's release,
The penitent mariner sounds with mapless gaze.
The deck's fog curries promises, and vents
Continuously an itinerary that recedes,
That cannot begin but in a choice to cease.
The makers of the world disguise alarm.
A perfect silence heeded in the calm
Breaks the array of broken images,
Ports swiftly in the south, sun's cargo grace.

To One Far Away

In all the world where are you?
Where will I find you?
Are you among the people
Perched upon that mountain beyond?
Can I perceive your form
Amongst the thronging of that
High and distant haze?

Where shall I go?
How have I let you fall from me,
And filter out among the wider paths
Of irretrievable Fate?
What snowy peak? What rock?
What island? Where do you live
The latter of your days? Among
What people innocent of your
Wild youth, your forgotten past,
Do you roam, speaking new languages,
Your image drunk by strange
And pale and radiant streets,
That know no limit to
Peaceful content in laying
Out their carpet for your grace?

New World

A new classicism,
Cut-throat in the cafe,
Scraps of rumpled poetry,
The professor knows.

Pomegranate newspapers abandoned
Take numbers from the lot,
Lazy stubs that stroll smoking
Thrown into the swan.

The great Indian funnel
Whose red eye roams
Drinks milk from their pockets
To whitewash the walls.

O dip of the sun-laced lash.

Habanera

Night of glass flowers,
blowing, blowing,
divergent from sleep.

The painted fruit of the facade,
Grandfather's open doors,
predict the trembling dawn.

And in the milky abyss
of silence to which all gathers,
the calendars bear no names.

Operatic resolve of arrival.
(No names for the flowers of ice,)
blowing, blowing...

Parade

These immensities of light there is no distance to
go as far as I would go, a bluejay on a wire.
There is no end to day, nor any end to light
that paints the buildings flat, mapped against themselves.
Through the brilliant trees, the tunnels momently
of avenue and ledge incite a new terrain
dim foreclosed from the crowd. The sweep and surge of things
extends only to you, the poplars' exploded fuse.
Shielded in each view a witness is concealed.
High in the solitude above the slow parade
the fountain in the day seizes your going by.
There is no corner round the city, is no end
to what the will believes, thrills, relieves, reveals.
Windows black and dim burn in the summer day;
the rivers of the leaves exhort the ancient swells
of travellers within. This silence is the same
as that within the stone in sunlight in the field.
Each is facade, attends upon your return.

Song

This ended movie
has its beauty
and the chinese music
playing is sick
at its endless
bedside duty:
the keeping awake
our one love
to reprove
age's senseless
forgetfulness.

So White

So white, the sunlight on the buildings
Compels the eye inward to distances,
Obsolete voyages, longing to recall
The immaculate sojourn at the heart of time.

The crowds move light as flies or paper
Through streets that rise to meet the sun;
What is unique on which the gaze is strung
That finds enough in simply being here,
Is the illumined shutter through which are flung
The different worlds, of beauty and despair.

La Vita Nuova

Banks of houses and rooftops murmur
Sidereal arrival of the dawn,
Worlds of isolated calendars
And promises days have no time to keep.
Identity, broken in the traveller,
Is radiance and the chatter of solemn words
Sympathetic over a range of mountaintops.

Island-ominous shadows, focused and spindled
Elude the eye's swift radiating answer...
As dark as absence seen before forgetting.

The Rose

Awakening from a slumbering dream
Upon the grass beneath a tree,
I spied the fissure of my realm
From that gone wandering with thee.

The painted boards that were before
Us laid out in that waiting scene
Like petals blossomed, dew covered,
Observed the atom of my dream.

Dark realms of earth to brinks of blades
Were hollow to my body's blaze.
The limit of the sluggish eye
Perceived the warbling cradle's veil.

I followed thee to where thy shroud
Slid up the portrait of the day,
Thy fruit's skin lively burgeoning,
And pressed my hole up to thy gate.

My blindness did not thee unrobe,
Nor fathomed how two minds could fill
One space converged by some keen fate
That understood the fullness there.

Emerging words within my soul
From some unknown and hidden source
In coruscating melody
Contrary to thy sphere did spin.

A cherry fell down from the tree.
Its hard fruit wounded swelled and swarmed
With life within its world to give.
Compelled, I likened it to thee.

Chasm

All of ash that's hauled by truck
Revises alleys in your sleep.

The harbour rumbled by the barge
that ropes you of its own accord
is fiery black on screens of time
ignited past the hour's bend.

The city's statue bleeds in fits,
revolving hours shattering
around that scene by men ignored,
rising hymn of time's instance.

Tankers with their skulls of steel
reel banners at the edge of day
that fill the holes of gaping eyes
with dreams, and leave more holes to fill.

Windows drink the hungry eye
where flashes jargon of the hill,
gold rings imposed on cakes of stone
in cool hours after the climb.

All of ash that's hauled by truck
Revises alleys in your sleep.

After Wartime

She has not been to war, but she can see
That he has been to war. They touch, they meet,
In darkness where he dreams his private nightmare.
He does not know that she has seen him sleep.

She, touched by the years of war, is lovely.
Sympathetic, she meets him mid-way on the stair,
Tailoring humour to his lack of tact,
Tailored by a lack of shoes on the shoe rack.

Her father, sore as a mirror after drinking,
Plumbs the depths of the years, one language, and one culture.
This is the way things end, and things begin.
A let-down shade lets sunlight in, and darkness.

Premonition of War

I

Awake, buttons as vows sealed.
On a holy day three poor men
Shall have plum brandy, cigars, pheasants,
And laugh at gluttony, and at death.

From the mouth of the golden horn,
A bouquet of triumphal soundings
In processional from our heart's fasting chamber,
A crown of jangling thorns inventing.

Those feats of devotion which duty deigns
Hover about us like solemn hatbands
Which we place on the table, by our gentle sleeves,
Relegated to the lush hatrack of our desires.

The languorous flesh, the heavy burden,
Laughter plies our sullen stew;
I kiss the brow of groaning appearance,
This day our bodies are hung with plums.

Friendship is a horse that smokes cigars
Garnered by portentous sudden poppy wreath
Chafed by tremulous potentialities
And laid to rest in soft mask's inverse.

Three men in a concert of souls,
With eyes divided by a hundred cities' dawns,
We drink flowing blood from the bowl of our three hearts
Where lions foam and wilt in watchful stone.

The crackle of silence devours my white shirt,
Spray of tallow, fingers of flame,
My grimacing heart a corpse with pockets full of gold
Ascending spiral stairs of milky glass.

My eyes are black moons
Beneath rising clouds of lids
That emerge like sabers wild and sullen
To cut the burdens of the creaking lemon trees.

The white breast of Venus lies severed on silver
Atop the bitter mantle that bites its moaning lip,
A white sail amassing stains
Above a cupboard that contains a thought.

Seated beside Dignity, Beauty admires
His ivory fingers recall the ancient terrain,
The tones and textures of earth's roaming cradle,
A senile toast, a quick and darting caprice.

Sonorous landscape of duels and crucifixions,
A tavern in voyage on the sea,
More sonorous than trees of ripened olives,
The perseverance of wounded and drunken accordions,
The arrival, swift and sudden, of ancient shores,
The long line at last reveals its melody.

An explorer who's come to the heart of his madness,
Flicking his peelings on the rug of lies,
Answers for himself with the voice of silence
Shuffling ignorance on the heath of despair.

Walking the ancient hall we await the dawn,
Troubled by white stones we had put to sleep,
Smoking our hearts like marble cigars,
Breath from the lips of our ancient dreams.

Where grains of mythic consternations bloom
Beneath the shadows of my bloody hands
Melting by the sombre flame of time
From banished brows young sweetness trickles down.

Beyond the drunken trellis beckon
Vines that creep in tangled solitude,
Intelligent expansions of the muse
Ever murmuring the compass of the night.

I saw the form of the only thing I ever loved,
The holy thing, at which I bowed my head in shame.
A sweetness demanding all our agony,
The only thing, at which I wept of shame.

The fire burns so bright in the death chamber.
All the colors have gathered in all the flowers.
And all scents, and all sensations.
And all tastes and sounds, and all hidden meanings.

Which burn through the heart, that knows all life,
The vigil in clay, love's sole quest,
Our guardian dress, our altar of jasmine,
The mansion of dreams, and the heart buried in heart.

These white tombs awakened in our sleep,
Who flutter in an endless night
On streaming winds of memory,
Fill absence with their solitude.

The strings of the lyre have blown away,
The soot of the angels covers the ground,
The tears of the vanquished hopes eternal
Live in the shadows of fluttering sound.

Cold winds on my cheek and the lemon trees
Tell me nothing and nowhere to go.
My heart is cut out and buried in the earth
Where the feet of unanswered lovers pace.

By the sea that laps the child full stone,
Where the palm fronds writhe in the wind's void,
The star's root shoots its shivering seed
Through the icy blood of your moonlit dreams.

The perfumed shells of your moon sought lids
Beat and breathe across the eyes of my heart
In the chamber numb and hourless
Where the memory of the world sleeps.

Angels churn in the face of the clock;
The minutes of your tresses tick;
Moonbeams creak, brought on ropes
To the trembling flesh of your sleepbound neck.

O, truth, what was it?
I found myself in strange cities, by the sea,
In the time that is held from us,
White mornings that I've always known,
And always you were there, or I looked for you.

I passed the form of man cragged in the rocks of red deserts,
Bone dry and niggardly, crushed beneath your soul,
Your gentle flesh, the sandal of perfumed harmony,
Heart of my quest, ancient globe in eternity's hand.

Perched above the urn of the world
Goats of famine roll their eyes.
Endless the milk is drained from the skies,
Endless the chaff is blown from the wheat.

In Mexico, horrible nights of white purity,
Sweating, I dreamed she was there too,
So close; I struggled with ancient nights
That told me nothing, O winds, and masks.

In winter, in a new city,
Patterning the rags and scents
Of solitude into a prayer,
The stillness of the bare new year
Falls empty in the hands of sound.

In silence we voyage to distant lands,
Charted by the boldness of our love,
Daring to defy the strict sound of death,
Holding tears to the whirling globe of eternity.

On the rooftop golden boats drag gentle rains,
The steady fall of tears of one who waits.
O Pity! O Boats of Charity!
We're in love and all night it's raining on our roof.
The rains are the tears of my love who is waiting to find me.

Voices you have carried with you across seas
Sound new to me like bells in a foreign city
Which begin to change their shape to you too
In morning's flaught of white when you tell them.

You are the mirror to my century,
And I to yours, spanning its length.
From all the portals of the world—
Time's thought drips, stains your chin.

I in my skinnen coat have wandered about the town,
Beneath the sun and starving, my two feet on the ground;
Sleepless and broke, I made my inn by the river,
And drank the stale cheery ale of the stink of the bank.

I labored under the sun, accomplicing slavery,
Moving the rocks that will outlive us all.
I saw the laborers on the roofs, the birds in the trees,
I lifted the rock that will crush the sun.

Baths of ale, red silken glimpses,
Jade towers, drink your wisdom.

I cut the grass whose cutting killed my fathers.
White rooftops gleam in series beneath the sun.
These tree-tops first seen by conquistadors
Have made a gift of hours to be pawned...

A mask lies on the poet's lawn.
Through spiders, violets, eternity draws its breath.
Sleep traced the conclusive dream of memory—
Where, white of sound, all ceasing times converge...

At foot of the mountain, I wait for your return,
All numbers and colors in posture rearranged.
The fluid newspaper of my heart
Shades sorrows from itself.

All the world exudes a sweetness
Awakening to my fading lips...

*

Where children played outside the hallowed walls
That dew-splayed sunlight crept up like ivy
And kept our laughter, the smoke of cheap cigars,
This was our university.

Where History rose within the glass
That towered before blind and furtive eyes
And wept its tears of day old crumbs,
This was our university.

Where the fruit ripe murmured on the vine
And breezes swayed gentle from the sea
And the leaves grew brown upon our boughs,
This was our university.

The muddy backyard where dark plums lay
In the cold, wet air where our thoughts strayed,
Where we drank dark wine while the moon danced,
This was our university.

Where sunbeams filled the resting grapes
In the handkerchief our hopes had draped
And spires of clouds our hearts climbed,
This was our university.

Where love was glimpsed between the slats
Where talking we had laid our hats,
And walked away when swung the gate,
This was our university.

On silent stages of the night,
Shades patterned to our feet,
We traversed byways of eternity,
Blind purveyors of ghostly brinks.

Who whispered to each other
On the icy fantastic ledge
Over the black bank of blinking signs—
Plucked petals of words.

*

Arm upright slender in the fleeing day
Shadows the basement where you wait for me.

In the chinaman's eye of the morning
Steel and concrete speed through your hands—
White blossoms of the battleship of the world
That departs in the immense ports of the skies—

Whose wings have slipped up through the pavement's cracks,
Beats voices of the crowd upon the sun,
Far caravans of stasis may concede...

Leak utterances of you up through cement...
Explicit and regardant without words
Tolls in the hollow bell within the world
Some alley where the day winds you away...

III

Beneath a yellow twilight stained blood red
I carry lemons in my pockets, wrapped in linen.
The somnolent voice of the wind through the boughs
Awakens the dancers of stone on the hill.

Beneath plums within shells of clasped withered hands,
On the wall, beneath the stars, by the fountain of Delphi,
Where the floe of my heart melts under the lilt of vines,
I look out to the sea and sing these Alegrias.

I would do anything to win your love.
Flags will hang from the wall on the day that you love me.
You can see them from the sea as your boat draws near.
If you don't like the flags I will change them.

—And always, through the world, while I may breathe—
I'll seek you through each repetitious street...
And in the timeless progress of the crowd,—
Your apparition I may chance to meet.

Where sunlight on white concrete climbs
In every crack I'll search your face.
I'll look for you behind each arcade stall,
Your restless childhood I might hope to trace.

I'll toss coins over the yellow balcony
On the day you wear your whitest dress.

IV

In the garden told by sun and moon,
The moon's ray touches my vat on the floor,
Speaking to the stars of spring to come,
In the afternoon a rainfall of decisions.

My afternoons embraced by the garden wall,
The rhythm speaks in the cat's appearance,
Announcing the task turning with the sun,
Turning with the world of a listening leaf.

Vine that creeps, that knows you,
Knows the absent life of your stained hand,
The forgotten leaf broken in the lake's water,
By the cool wind that rumpled the swan's neck.

Food is the mouth, Voice is the hunger,
The place that you stop is the face that you make,
The things that we need are our secret larder,
We're moving, Always, towards our resting place.

The sun overhead is the hand on the shoulder,
The pink citrus memory pointing the way,
Below, the moon stubborn in the face of withdrawal,
Rising the sap through the bending of ways.

An hour of water, sheaf of the sun,
Rolls prophecies through the gut of the streets,
While we bathe in a glimpse of a corner revealed,
Welled in the pockets that have deigned us to keep.

Our shoes, barometers of the turning tide,
Our coat, hung whispered message sly,
Hour of meditation wrapping its robe,
Suiting action to break voice on wet repose.

The vat, stirred, stirring, in our absence,
Rain drawing light to our scraggly hide,
Ascending, a ring of dough circles the spiring city,
Landing light on our collar through breaking sky.

All through the city, Silence, golden light,
Wherefore our shoes deign not speak a word,
Brought light, brought silence, Awakeness,
What message uttered in stirring heart.

Go, return, you who have come,
Find home in a heap where you've found breath,
Dawning on placid lakes utterances of hunger,
First stirrings removed of invisible shells.

A stone, ringlets, waves moving outwards,
Trembling leaf of resolution dawn.
Hand moving outwards, shaken of sorrow,
Sleep, exhausted, embraced by the dawn.

V

Baths of milk, apparition of fountains,
Possible issue of your stone trapeze...

Naked, arrows in the bow of Charity,
We stood atop the rooftop of the world,
When all residual echoed in the wind
Whose unfettered departure gleamed.

Turned of the moon, coin of the sun,
Slapped on the forearm of a river confederate;
A chessboard at the rocking wooden eyebrow's elbow,
Through the sailing arrows of the ancestral tower.

Glory, waken joyous on golden balconies,
Swimming 'midst the fragrant crowds,
A toast, golden beams in the naked palm,
A new edition wakes to the endless river.

What leafs such senses have brought to life,
Flowing in the trampled bouquet,
A gift of resolution, from the tower,
Joins the tidings of the parade.

The new thought comes in a burst of vision
That clears the table by the foaming sea
Dropping the fruit of recurrent image
Setting our course on a timeless sea

O, When to those new shores we arrive!
We shall ravage bitterness, with liberty
Where fertile soils await our patient seed;
Then we shall be the first to know our time.